Candy Crush Saga

Advanced Guide

Tyler Davis & Emily Jackson

Disclaimer

Quick View of the Guide

Have you been stuck on a level for a couple of days now and feel like you won't be able to pull through it?? Well, you don't have to stop playing your favorite game just because you are stuck on some obstacle-filled tricky level.

Just skim through this book and you are surely going to find the solution inside. This is not any ordinary Candy Crush Guide. If you are a beginner, then refer to the prequel of this book **"Candy Crush Saga: Tips, Cheats, Secrets and Strategies!!"**. That book will tell you all you need to know about the game, the basic game modes, obstacles, perks and general tips to play the game.

This book **"Candy Crush Saga: Advanced Users Only!!"** is specifically meant for advanced level players who are already quite far on their Candy Crush journey.

Being a Candy Crush fan, by now you must have an idea about how the level of difficulty increases as you progress with the game. Here you will find some amazing tips and cheats to pull through some of the trickiest levels of the game.

This book contains some of the most exclusive hints and tricks. You won't find them anywhere else as most of the tips and cheats mentioned here been taken from the experience of some expert Candy Crush players who have already succeeded the game.

So don't just stop here. Keep on reading and find a solution to clear the level you are stuck on.

Table of Contents

Introduction

The fact that you are still reading this book is proof enough that you are an avid player of the highly addictive Candy Crush Saga. Needless to say that Candy Crush Saga is not an ordinary matching game. The levels and obstacles keep on getting trickier as you progress. Basic tips and cheats seem insufficient to beat the challenges and achieve the targets in higher levels.

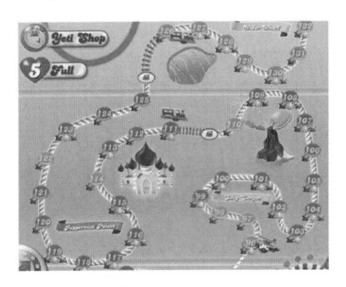

Well, this book caters specifically to the advanced level difficulties of the game. But before we move on to the more advanced level tricks and hints, let's just quickly go through the prequel of this book.

Highlights of the Previous Guide

The prequel of this book **"Candy Crush Saga: Tips, Cheats, Secrets and Strategies!!"** is all about the basics of Candy Crush Saga. The book starts with an overview of the game, including some incredible statistics and a bit about the story line. The purpose of the game is to help

Mr. Toffee and the cutie pie Tiffi Toffee in their quest to travel the world. They meet different characters and face several sweet but deadly obstacles that hinder their colorful journey.

Apart from the amazing storyline, there are several other factors that make Candy Crush Saga different from other matching games. We assume you already know about these factors. All the unique features of the game are elaborated in detail in the previous version of this book.

Summing up, a different story and characters in every episode, increasingly challenging targets, colorful obstacles, candylicious perks and different strategies to clear the five game modes are some of the uncountable features that stand Candy Crush Saga apart from its rivals.

Other than the overview, story line and distinct features, the prequel of this book contains detailed explanations about the following:

The Playing Technique: The basic playing mechanism of Candy Crush Saga is the same as any other ordinary matching game. You have to make combinations of three or more candies to attain the required score. However, the strategy to play the game is not the same. You need to plan your moves according to the requirements and limitations of the specific level.

Game Modes: There are five modes of Candy Crush Saga; namely moves and score mode, jelly mode, ingredient mode, timed levels and Candy Order levels. The Candy Order mode appears quite later in the game and is therefore a part of this advanced version.

Special Candies: Make combinations of more than 3 candies and in different patterns to get a special candy. There are four types of special candies; vertically striped, horizontally striped, wrapped candy and color bomb. Each has its own unique properties and features. Special candies become a necessity in some advanced levels. We will talk about them later on in this book.

Sweetly Deadly Obstacles: Obstacles are one of the most enticing and addictive feature of Candy Crush Saga. As the name suggest, these are impediments that make a level more challenging and difficult to clear. These include stone squares, tornadoes, chocolates, licorice, locked candies and many others. Time bomb is one of the most deadly obstacles. It destroys the entire candy board and makes you lose the level if you don't diffuse it within the given number of moves.

Charms and Boosters: These are power ups that help you clear the tricky levels. You can buy them from the Yeti shop. Every charm and booster has something different to offer and helps you in one way or another. Buy a charm once and it will stay with you throughout the game, whereas Boosters are for one time use only. However you can buy them as many times as you want from the Yeti shop.

Tips, Tricks and Cheats: This is the most fun and amazing part of the prequel. Here we have disclosed several secrets and cheats that are meant to help you progress in the game more quickly. The most amazing trick is on how to increase the number of lives without paying for them. In this section you will find several tips and tricks that will make your gaming experience even more entertaining and enjoyable.

The prequel also contains an FAQ section and good news for Candy Crush fans.

What's New?

Well, that was just a wrap of the previous section. The purpose of summarizing the basic version of the book prior to moving on to the advanced one is to warm you up a little before getting started with the trickier part.

Moving forward, the basic story line is the same. Mr. Toffee and the darling Tiffi Toffee are on the same quest. Just as they move on in their journey, they come across several new obstacles at the same time. These are so deadly and challenging that they get stuck in some levels for a couple of days and even weeks in some cases.

Well this was to be expected, wasn't it? Every Candy Crush player knows that the levels will keep on getting more difficult as they move on with the game. So, what is new?

Well, here is the catch. Do you actually know what difficulties you are going to face and how to deal with them? As you move on to higher levels, you will encounter a new game mode and some new types of obstacles. There are some specific levels that are notorious in the Candy Crush arena. These are the trickiest levels of the game so pick your moves VERY carefully.

We will discuss it all in the upcoming chapters. Let's start by exploring the advanced modes of the game.

Advanced Game Modes and Levels

Apart from the moves and score, timed, jelly and ingredient modes, there is another game mode of Candy Crush Saga known as the Candy Order mode. The first level of this mode is unlocked in the Wafer Wharf episode at level 126.

Candy Order Levels

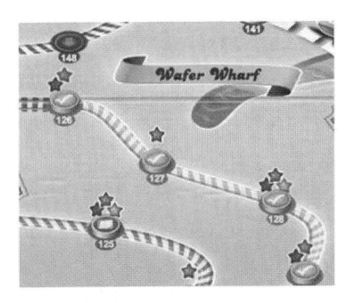

Candy Order Levels are denoted by pink circles on the level selection map. This is the favorite mode of most Candy Crush fans. In Candy Order levels, you are required to fulfill certain orders in order to clear that level. These are the most uncertain type of levels. You never know what orders you are going to get in the next one. The orders are like a surprise for the players and this is what makes Candy Order the most fun and addictive mode of the game.

The collect orders keep on changing at every level and you need to devise your playing strategy accordingly. The image given below is a snapshot of level 126. As you can see from the collect orders, here you are required to crush 20 red, 20 green and 20 blue candies.

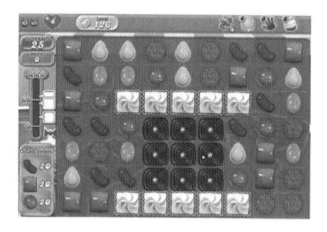

This is the first and easiest level of Candy Order mode. Don't think it will be a piece of cake though! Here are other examples just to give you an idea of how difficult the collect orders can be.

Multiple Obstacles

We talked about obstacles in the previous book. As an advanced level player, you must have had to deal with spreading chocolate, locked candies or time bombs in certain levels. How about dealing with several deadly obstacles at the same time in the same level? Well this is going to happen in the advanced levels. As you move on with the game, you will come across several levels where you will have to deal with more than three or four obstacles.

The above image is an ideal example of a multiple obstacle level. Here you have to deal with time bombs, tornadoes, teleports, stone squares, and meringues of four different kinds. All in all, this level contains eight obstacles making it eight times more difficult to clear.

The Deadlier Obstacles

You are already aware of the blockers and obstacles that impede your progress and make it difficult to clear the level. Well, here are some more of them that you will encounter in higher levels.

Tornadoes

The tornadoes are one of the most thrilling obstacles of Candy Crush Saga. They are quite deadly and do not subside by themselves. You do not have any control over them. Adding to the difficulty is the fact that tornadoes hit randomly. You never know which candies the tornado will hit next.

This can make planning moves and making special candies a bit tricky. Suppose you lined up several candies to create special candy effects and suddenly the tornado smacked one of them. Your entire plan will go to waste as well as the number of moves that you used to execute it.

And the destruction does not stop here! It does not only attack candies randomly; it also leaves behind a battered tile for one more move.

As you can see in the image above, the tornado created several cracked tiles. It will stay this way for one more move, thereby giving you fewer candies to crush.

Unfortunately, there is not much that you can do to get rid of them. The only way to deal with these deadly tornadoes is to analyze their movement and plan your moves accordingly.

Time Bomb Maker

As the name suggests, it creates the deadly time bombs. It makes an entire lane of time bombs. Time Bomb maker is eternal just like chocolate maker. It stays till the end of the level. You cannot get rid of it; you will have to destroy the bombs that it makes. Now you need to plan your moves in such a way that you diffuse the time bombs and achieve targets at the same time. Keep a balance between the two parameters or else you will fail the level and lose a life.

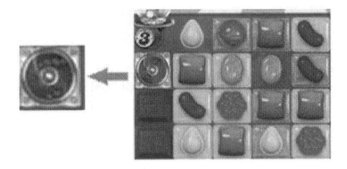

Here is a tip for playing moves and score level or timed level having a time bomb maker. Strategize your moves so that you diffuse as many time bombs as possible. In these levels, your first priority and main focus should be to crush time bombs. This would work in two ways: 1). You will get rid of the obstacle and 2) You will get closer to your score target as every time bomb you destroy will raise the score bar by 3000 points.

Multi Layered Meringue

Meringue was there in the initial levels as well. The first meringue was introduced in level 21 and it is the simplest type of meringue, a white creamy like tile that can be removed very easily. However, the Meringue keeps on coating layers on itself as you move on to higher levels.

The number of layers represents the number of times that you will have to break a candy adjacent to a meringue to get rid of it completely. Apart from the one layer meringue that makes its first appearance in Level 21, there are several other types that you will encounter in advanced levels.

Two-layer Meringue: This silver layered meringue is introduced in level 111 which is the first level of Peppermint palace episode. You need to hit it twice to get rid of it and make space for a candy.

Three-layer Meringue: Making its first appearance in the first level of Gingerbread Glade which is level 141, this meringue looks like a white and brown chocolate square. The first hit would break the brown block and two more hits would destroy it completely.

Four-layer meringue: Appearing first in the Cupcake circus episode at level 171, this meringue takes four adjacent candy crushes to destroy it. It has a silver square over the layer of brown block as illustrated in the image below.

Five-layer meringue: This is the most difficult and deadly meringue which makes its official first appearance in level 276. We say official because in some games, it may also come as a surprise such as in level 231. The fifth layer is the brown circular spot in the centre of the tile. It takes the highest number of hits to get off the board.

Meringues can be troublesome in jelly levels. You need to first make a couple of hits to destroy the meringue and then a few more to crush the jelly.

Advanced Level Perks

As you progress in the game, the level of difficulty increases. The darling Yeti is aware of your difficulties and unlocks one more booster in advanced levels, other than the ones already explained in the previous book.

Lucky Candies

The first Lucky Candy is unlocked at level 130. It is the candy with a tick on it. This Booster needs to be activated before the game starts.

Lucky candies can be used in Candy Order levels only. Once you activate it, it will show up in any color on your candy board. Match it with the same colored normal candies and it will turn into a special candy. It is not necessary to combine more than 3 candies to create a special candy. A combination of two regular and one same colored lucky candy would also get you a special candy.

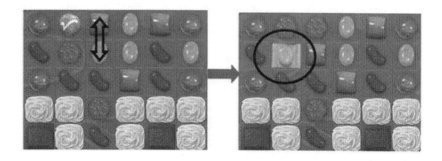

Now which special candy the lucky candy will transform into is pure luck. You never know whether you will get a striped candy, wrapped candy or may get lucky enough to get a color bomb.

Train Stuck Between the Two Stations

How many times have you been stuck on any level for quite a few days? Or weeks may be! Well you are not the only one who gets stuck on a level after every few levels. This is faced by all the Candy Crush fans. The pattern of the levels is such that you get an extremely difficult level after every few comparatively easy levels.

The game has been designed in such a way that your candylicious train is sure to get stuck between two stations. It goes like this. In every episode, there are a few consecutive levels that are quite easy and you will be able to clear them in one attempt. And then you will come across a level that will keep you hooked for endless days. These are the notorious levels of Candy Crush Saga. The gap between two notorious levels keeps on getting smaller as you move on to advanced level episodes.

In the upcoming section, you will find some useful tips that will help you clear the trickiest levels of the Saga. Later on in this book, we have identified some notorious levels and have written some specific tips pertaining to those levels only.

Tricks to Clear the Trickiest Levels

Create Multiple Color Combinations

Tasty, divine and delicious are attributes that you get for making several combinations in one move. Obviously it is not possible for any player to make more than one combination in one move. Then how do you think you will get yourself a divine candy crush. Luck, it may be!

But you cannot rely on pure luck in advanced levels. Well here is the tip. Observe every possible move on the board and try to find out which candies will replace the place of crushed candies. Plan your moves such that one combination creates several subsequent combinations.

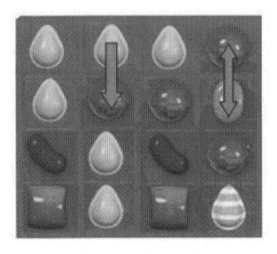

The above image is one such example of multiple combinations. Here if you move the blue candy down, the yellow candy will come down itself thereby making another combination in the same move.

Make Smart Use of the Special Candies

Don't rush in using your special candies. Use them in such a way as they help you reach the target of the specific level. For example, in jelly levels where jellies are clustered together, wrapped candies are a smart choice. Try to create them in between the jelly cluster. Even if you create a wrapped candy a couple of candies away from the cluster, don't rush in bursting the wrapped candy. First bring it near the huddle of jellies and then explode it.

The image below is a snapshot of level 99. As you can see in this image, jellies are locked in the centre of the candy board. Wrapped candy explosion near this colorful bunch will get you several jellies in one move.

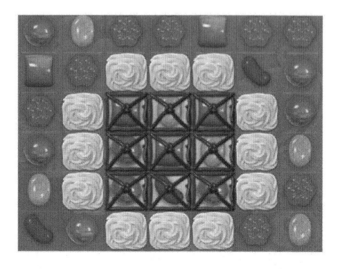

This is another example of a jelly level. Here a vertically striped candy will be more helpful as compared to a wrapped candy. A vertical striped special candy on top of the meringue row will clear all the meringues in one swipe.

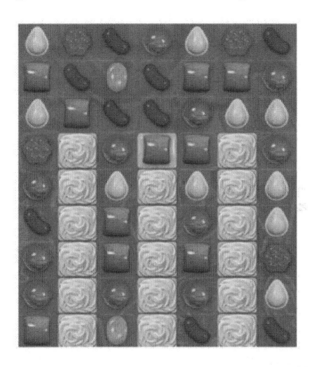

Waste Time in Timed Levels

Waste the time in timed levels only when there is a time bomb and you have already achieved your target score. Don't take a risk with the time bomb. If it explodes, you will fail the level regardless of achieving the required score.

Reshuffle the Candies For Free

You already know about the shuffle candy that can be used any time during a level to shuffle the candy board.

Well, here is a small cheat for Android users to shuffle their candy board without paying for the shuffle candy. However, unlike shuffle candy this trick can be used at the start of the level only.

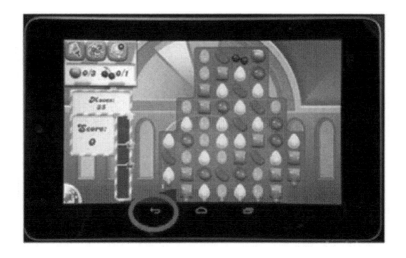

As soon as a level starts, observe the candy board and if you don't like the placement of candies, tap the back button on your device. It will take you back to the level selection map without using a life. This trick is extremely helpful in time bomb levels.

For example, as you can see in the below image it is quite difficult to crush the time bomb. If you come across this level on your Android phone, you may go back to the level map and then play the level again. You might get the same colored candies next to the time bomb.

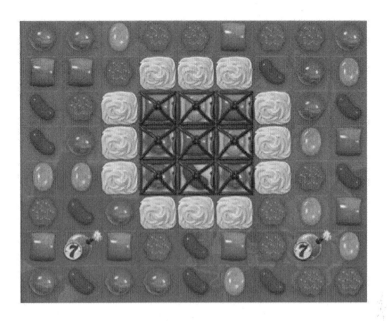

Just remember two things.

1. You can go back to the level selection map prior to making any moves. Once you make a move, then going back to the map will cost you a life.

2. This trick is not applied in timed mode. So don't waste your time in observing the board. You can observe the board for the purpose of planning the moves. The "Pause Timed Levels Candylicious secret" in the prequel of this book explains the process of pausing and observing the timed levels.

Save the Gifts

Your may have been getting lives and +3 moves booster gifts from your friends. Do you accept them the moment you get them? Well, if you do so then you are wasting your gifts.

If you accept the +3 moves booster without giving a second thought then the gift can only be used in that particular level. For example, if you received a +3 moves booster while you are on level 104, then you can use this booster in this particular level only.

However, the same does not apply in case of lives. Accept the lives only when you are out of lives. Do not accept the life gift when your life pack is already full. Let them stay in your message box. You can use them at anytime and at any level.

Know the Obstacles

It is very important to analyze the obstacles before you start making any moves. For example, the time bomb should be your first priority no matter how many other obstacles are there. Striped candies are the best and in most cases, the only way to deal with time bomb maker.

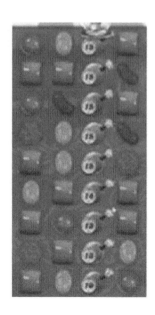

Similarly, striped combo combinations and wrapped candy combinations are the best way to get rid of licorices and locked candies. In case of the rainbow candy, observe its changing color pattern and then plan your moves accordingly. Every obstacle has a different property and needs to be destroyed in a different way.

Chocolate and Time Bomb

Here is another secret for you. You may hate the Candy Crush chocolate for the fact that it spreads so quickly. But after knowing this secret you may start loving the chocolate in some specific levels. Chocolate eats up the time bomb. In levels when the time bomb is located next to the chocolate and the chocolate is spreading in the direction of the bomb, there are high chances that the chocolate will eat up the time bomb.

It does not mean that you should not try to destroy the bomb. Don't take the risk and crush the bomb if you can. However, if you think it's absolutely impossible to crush the bomb and that it will explode anyway then make moves far away from the chocolate. Don't break the chocolate or else it will stop spreading. Make random moves without crushing the chocolate and you never know, this notorious obstacle may turn in your favor.

Take this chance only when you can not find any other way of destroying the time bomb.

Check the Level before You Toggle

Not all boosters can be used in all levels. For example, Lucky candy can be used in Candy Collect levels only. Similarly, Jelly Fish Booster can be activated in jelly levels only. The boosters applicable to a particular level are displayed on the opening screen of a level from where you can toggle it on/off.

The image below represents the opening screen of level 100. As you can see, you can use three boosters in this level. The ones that are not applicable in this level are blocked.

The important thing to note here is that you should always play a level at least once without using any booster. Check the difficultly of the level and then decide if and which booster you will need to clear the particular level.

The Secret behind Tornado

In the obstacles section of this book, we introduced you to the deadly tornadoes. As per the rules, the only way to deal with tornadoes is to plan your moves around them. But what about deviating slightly from the rules to make the game more fun and interesting? Well here is another secret that you will help you deal with the thrilling tornadoes.

After the tornado attacks, the damaged tile remains unusable for one more move. However, the destructed tile heals itself immediately after the next move. The little secret here is that the candy above the destructed tile will move down in place of the healed tile.

Another secret is that tornadoes do not attack the same tile more than once. Now that you know which candies will replace the healed tile and it won't be damaged again, plan your moves accordingly.

Tips To Get Through the Advanced Jelly Levels

Jelly mode is considered to be the most difficult amongst them all. Some of the most notorious levels of Candy Crush Saga are Jelly levels. Following are some of the tips that will help you clear the tricky jelly levels.

Save Your Fish

Resist the urge to use Jelly fish in Jelly levels. Clear away the easy jellies by making candy combinations. Use the fish for clearing the jellies located at difficult-to-reach places like next to any obstacle or in the corners. Each jelly fish eats up 3 jellies. Therefore save the jelly fish for the three most difficult jellies of the particular level.

Eat the Chocolate

Chocolates are real trouble in Jelly levels. They increase the number of crushes required to clear the jelly. In normal circumstances you would have to crush the jelly twice to get rid of it. However, a chocolate covered jelly increases that number up to three. First you need to break the chocolate and then the jelly underneath.

In jelly levels, try to break the chocolate as quickly as

possible. Most importantly, try to keep the chocolate from spreading over to the jelly tile. Every time a jelly tile gets coated by a chocolate, it will increase the number of crushes required to clear the jelly.

Don't Opt For Singles

Don't opt for single combinations in jelly levels. Try to create as many special candies as possible. And most importantly, resist the urge to burst the special candies. In most of the higher jelly levels, mere special candies would not suffice enough to clear all the jellies. Create several special candies and then swap them together. Wrapped-striped, color Bomb-striped and wrapped-wrapped are the best and highly explosive special candy combinations.

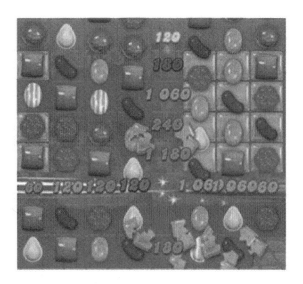

Tips To Get Through the Advanced Ingredient Levels

Ingredients are comparatively easy and the most fun levels to play. However, some of the advanced ingredient levels are extremely difficult and challenging. Try to follow these tips and you might pull off these levels easily.

Create Vertically Striped Candies

Vertically striped candies are the power-up for ingredients levels. Create a vertical striped candy in the row of the ingredient. Combine it with matching candies and it will take the ingredient down in one swipe.

In levels where ingredients are blocked by certain obstacles, even then the vertically striped candies are the best way to clear the level.

The image below is the snapshot of level 152. In this level, three layered Meringues are blocking the path of ingredients. If you crushed candies adjacent to the meringues, it would definitely de-layer the meringue and would bring the ingredient down. However, this simple strategy would make it almost impossible to get down 4 ingredients in 50 moves, which is the requirement of this level.

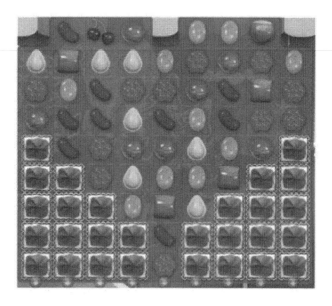

Three swipes of a vertically striped candy will clear all the meringues off that row. It is not possible to create vertically striped candies every time in every row. However, this should be your first priority.

Crush candies next to the meringues and below the ingredients as you would do in any other level. But in this specific level, instead of crushing meringues and wasting three moves to crush one three layered meringue, focus more on creating vertically striped special candies. Three strokes of this special candy and the ingredient in that row will cascade down to the bottom.

Transport through Teleports

In ingredients level with teleports, your first strategy is to observe the entry and exit points of teleports. Make a couple of moves and find out the exit point of the ingredient. Now instead of making combinations beneath the ingredient, crush candies beneath the teleport located above the exit point. This will automatically transport the ingredient to the exit point.

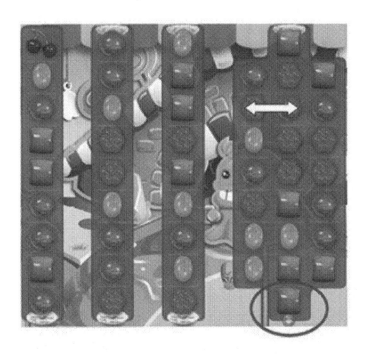

In the above image, there is only one exit point and the ingredient is far away from it. Try to make combinations as close to the exit point as possible. This will bring the ingredient closer to the exit point.

Forget About the Chocolate

In the Jelly mode, you should always keep an eye on the chocolate and try to keep it away from the jelly tiles. The same does not apply in case of ingredients levels. Chocolates are a concern only if they block the ingredient from getting to the bottom. Even then a single swipe of vertically striped candy would break the chocolate and ingredient out of the exit point in the same move. Don't waste your moves in breaking the chocolate. Let it spread if it is moving in the opposite direction of the ingredients. Just focus on getting the ingredients down.

Special Candies Only

There are certain levels in Candy Crush that can be cleared by creating special candies only. Following are two examples of such levels just to give you an idea on how to deal with them. You will come across several "special candies only" levels where special candies are the only solution to clear the level.

Level 77

As you can see in the image below, the jellies are located in the middle column which is isolated from rest of the candy board. Create vertically striped candies in the upper and lower part of the candy grid and crush them. The vertical crush will also hit the jelly in the center row.

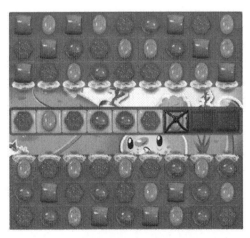

Level 138

Level 138 of Candy Crush Saga is another example of a 'Special Candies Only' level.

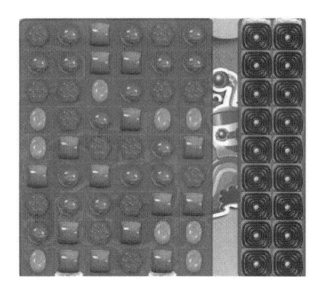

In this level, the jellies are underneath the licorice in two isolated columns. A horizontally striped candy is the only solution to clear away the licorice and reach the isolated jellies.

The Hardest Levels of Candy Crush Saga

In this section of the book, we have identified some of the trickiest and notorious levels of Candy Crush Saga. Following are some friendly tips that will help you clear these levels.

Secret to Clear Level 135

Level 135 is a candy collect order level. The secret here is that the collect orders are different on mobile phone Candy Crush Saga and Candy Crush Saga on Facebook. On a smart phone, the collect orders are to make and explode two wrapped-wrapped candies combos. On Facebook, the orders are to create and burst 6 wrapped candies. The Facebook version does not require you to make special candy combinations.

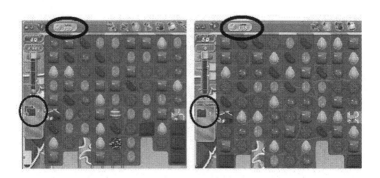

Now decide which one is easier for you. Usually the players find the Facebook version easier then the phone version. It is comparatively easy to create 6 wrapped candies rather than creating one wrapped candy and then saving it from getting crushed till you create another one next to it.

Tips to Clear Level 269

Level 269 is one of most challenging jelly levels. To clear this level, break the ice first to awake the fish inside. Don't use it immediately but break the ice just to keep the fish ready for use. Now plan your moves in such a way that you get striped candies. Burst the striped candies to get rid of licorice. The rest depends upon the fish and the candies that will appear next to the time bomb.

Tips to Clear Level 275

This is the first level where you will encounter the lethal time bomb maker. This is one of the deadlier obstacles of Candy Crush Saga as it creates an entire row or column of time bombs.

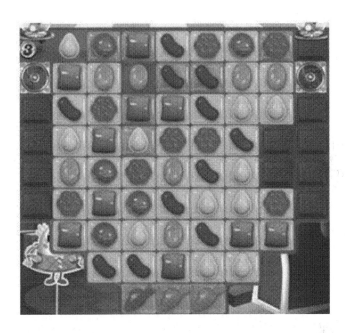

There are two strategies to clear this level.

1. Break the ice and awake the fish inside. Clear all the jellies except for the ones surrounding the bomb maker. Leave the surrounding jellies to be gulped by the fish.

2. Break the ice and free the fish inside it. The fish might break the chocolate at the top and will tell you if it's possible to destroy the time bomb or not. If not, quit the level and restart it. This will save your playing time.

Level 275 is one of the most difficult levels of the Saga. It will take a lot of tries to clear this one.

Tips to Clear Level 285

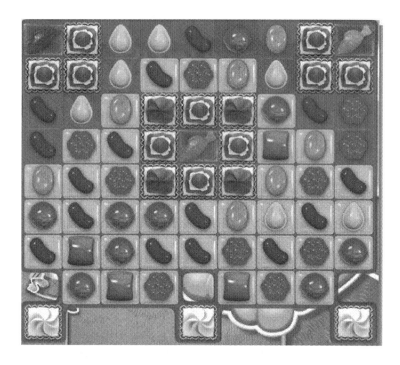

In this level, the most difficult jellies to clear are the three double jellies on the bottom of the grid. The only way to pull off this level is to first clear all other jellies except for the bottom three. Then use jelly fish to hit the bottom jellies through the wall. You are going to need six fish to break the three double jellies. Try to create a color bomb and swap it with a jelly fish. This will get you nine fish on the candy board. Use six to hit the bottom three jellies and three for any other remaining jellies.

Tips to Clear Level 342

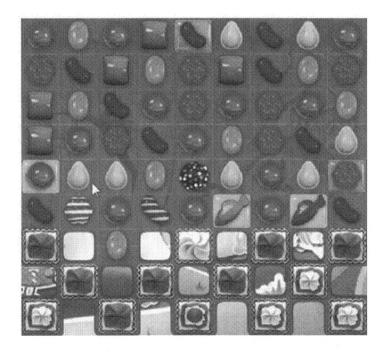

Level 342 is another highly notorious and challenging level of Candy Crush Saga. This is due to the fact that the jellies in this level are hidden under some of the meringues. The placement of jellies under the meringues is random in every game of level 342. There is no way of telling which of the meringues are hiding a jelly underneath them.

The only way to clear this level is to save the fish till the end of the level. Only the fish know which meringues have jellies hidden under them. Clear all other jellies and let the fish take care of the hidden ones. They will hit the right tile.

Don't waste the fish in taking the easier jellies. Don't even try to guess and clear the hidden jellies by yourself; there is no way you can do that within the limited moves allowed.

Try to clear the top few lines of meringues. It will make the remaining meringues comparatively easy to clear away. Create mega combos and special candy explosions. Match a fish to a rainbow sprinkle and it will produce several other fish on the candy board.

Avoid matching the fish with the same colored candies. You will be able to clear this level only if you could save the fish till you clear all the other jellies. If you must match the fish, then swap it with special candies so that you have some left for the hidden jellies.

Tips to Clear Level 417

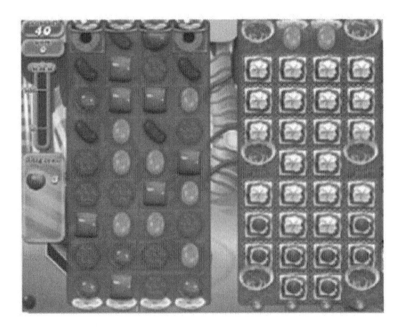

Level 417 is an ingredient level but the jellies are also there to protect the donut from tornado hits. In this particular level, the tornadoes can also destroy the pink candy donut once the jelly is cleared. So if you are not ready to use the pink donut, then don't remove the jelly off it. The donut is safe from the tornado as long it is wrapped inside the jelly. Once you break the jelly off the pink donut, make sure to use it in the next move. If you do not use them, the tornadoes will destroy the donut within the next one or two moves.

Win the Candylicious Fight!!

Candy Crush Saga that starts off as a sweet and simple Candy matching game turns into a thrilling and colorful Candylicious fight in higher levels. Since you are already an avid player, you must have an idea of the increasing level of difficulties as you progress with the game. This book will make all the challenging levels fun and interesting to play.

In most of the advanced levels, you need a lucky set of starting and interrelated subsequent combinations to clear the level. The most important thing that goes for all of the levels is the use of special candies. You should know which ones are appropriate for a particular level, when to create them and what special candy combos are required to clear the specific level.

This book explains the usage of special candies in detail by giving examples of several levels. It tells you some exclusive tips and secrets that you won't find anywhere else online. The last and most important tip that we would give you is to be patient and determined. There are some levels where you will get stuck for days or even weeks! Don't quit playing your favorite game just because you are unable to pull off a level.

With this book as your expert gaming companion, you are surely going to enjoy even the most notorious levels of this Saga.

Have Fun!!

Printed in Great Britain
by Amazon